The front cover

Read the title together, noting the plural 's' on the end of 'Shoemaker'.

How has the original story been changed? (*there are two shoemakers*)

Who is on the cover? (*the two shoemakers – Mollie and Ollie*) Which is which?

The back cover

Let's read the blurb.

Where does the help come from for Mollie and Ollie's shoemaking?

The title page

Re-read the title.

What sort of story do you think this is? (*A traditional tale.*)

Read the author's and illustrator's names.

READ

Read pages 2 to 5

Purpose: To find out why Mollie and Ollie were poor.

PAUSE

Pause at page 5

What do you notice about the way the story is written? (*It's written in rhyming verses.*)

Re-read this verse with the children to establish the rhythm of each line.

Which are the rhyming words on pages 2 to 5? (*together, leather; more, poor; bed, said*). Which lines of each verse are they on? (*second and fourth*)

Mollie and Ollie made very good shoes.
They lived and worked together.
To make good shoes they had to use
the very softest leather.

The cost of leather went up and up.
They had no money for more.
The very last pair of shoes was sold.
Now Mollie and Ollie were poor.

A bit of red leather was all they had.
They shut the shop and went to bed.

"No money for leather, no leather for shoes.
We've nothing to sell," they said.

READ

Read pages 6 to 9

Purpose: To think about why Ollie and Mollie did not know who made the shoes.

PAUSE

Pause at page 9

When did the elves come? (*in the night*)

When did Ollie and Mollie discuss the shoes? (*the next morning*)

What do the words 'snipped' and 'stitched' mean? (page 6)

Ask the children to read pages 8 and 9 with expression. Use a questioning and appreciative tone for Ollie and a surprised tone for Mollie's words.

In the night, six elves came in.
They sat down in a row.
They snipped the leather and stitched some shoes,
the finest they could sew.

"Did you make these shoes, dear Mollie?
They're lovely!" Ollie said.

"It wasn't me!" said Mollie,
"I was asleep in my bed."

5

READ

Read pages 10 and 11

Purpose: To find out what the rich man has to say.

PAUSE

Pause, at page 11

What does the rich man order and why does he want so many shoes? Why did he ask Ollie to make them? What is the problem for Mollie and Ollie?

READ

Read pages 12 and 13

Purpose: To find out what Mollie and Ollie thought about the problem of making a hundred pairs of shoes.

PAUSE

Pause at page 13

What was Mollie worried about? What did Ollie suggest?

Find the word on page 13 that means the same as 'great'? (*splendid*)

A rich man came and bought the shoes.
"You make good shoes," he said.
"Here is the money to make some more.
Make me a hundred pairs in red."

"They must be made by Friday noon
for that's my wedding day,
and if those pairs of shoes are late,
I shall refuse to pay."

Ollie said yes, they would make them!
But Mollie said, "What shall we do?
We'll never make a hundred pairs
in time, just me and you."

"Mollie, I wonder who made those shoes,"
said Ollie, "Let's hide tonight and see.
Whoever made those might make some more.
How splendid that would be."

READ

Read pages 14 to 17

Purpose: To find out if Ollie's idea will work.

PAUSE

Pause at page 17

How do Mollie and Ollie find out who has been making the shoes?

Let's recite the song the elves sang as they work.

Which pairs of words rhyme? (*stitch/rich; Ollie/Mollie; snip/clip; well/sell*) Do they look the same as well as sound the same?

Late that night they hid themselves.
They peeped from behind the door.
They saw six snipping, clipping elves,
all sitting on the shoe shop floor.

They sang this song, "New shoes to stitch,
a hundred pairs will make them rich.
Let's all snip and clip and stitch them well.
Mollie and Ollie need shoes to sell."

READ

Read pages 18 to 21

Purpose: To find out what Mollie did to reward the elves.

PAUSE

Pause at page 21

What is the problem for the elves when they work so late at night? What does Mollie do to help them?

Can anyone read out the part that tells us why Mollie made the clothes?

What do the words 'heeled' and 'soled' mean? (page 18)

For seven nights they stitched and snipped.
The shoes were heeled and soled.
But as they stitched, they shivered,
for the shoe shop floor was cold.

So Mollie made them little coats
to stop the elves from freezing,
and little caps and matching scarves,
in case they started sneezing.

READ

Read pages 22 to the end

Purpose: To predict the ending and see if the predictions are correct. What do you think will happen at the end?

PAUSE

Pause at page 24

Were your predictions right?

How do the shoemakers feel at the end of the story?

Which words tell you the elves are very happy with their caps, coats and scarves? (*cried with joy*)

The elves got dressed and cried with joy,
"We're warm, all thanks to you!"

22

Mollie and Ollie sold all the shoes.
Now they are rich and happy too.

24

After Reading

Revisit and Respond

T Ask the children to compare this version with other versions of the same story they have read. Ask them to identify the similarities and differences.

T Ask them to compare this story with *The Cherokee Little People* (also Purple Level) and identify the theme that is common to both.

T Ask the children in groups to practise and recite this rhyming story to the class, with one child acting as Ollie, one as Mollie, another as the rich man, and the rest as the elves.

W Ask them to look at page 13 and think of words they could use instead of 'splendid' (synonyms), e.g. *great, excellent, wonderful, brilliant,* etc.

W Ask them to find words in the story with the long phoneme 'or' in words from the text, noting different spellings (e.g. *more, floor, door*).

Follow-up

Independent Group Activity Work

This book is accompanied by two photocopy masters, one with a reading focus, and one with a writing focus, which support the main teaching objectives of this book. The photocopy masters can be found in the Planning and Assessment Guide.

PCM 25 (*reading*)

PCM 26 (*writing*)

Writing

Guided writing: Write the rhyming story as a prose version.

Extended writing: Write your own version of this story, with elves or fairies coming to sort out a problem. How would you reward them?

Assessment Points

Assess that the children have learnt the main teaching points of the book by checking that they can:

- read and explore a familiar traditional tale in poetry form
- discuss and compare stories with a common theme and different versions of the same story
- identify and discuss patterns of rhythm and rhyme
- read and write words with the long phoneme 'or'.